Massachusetts

Rich Smith

Visit us at
www.abdopublishing.com

Published by ABDO Publishing Company, 8000 West 78th Street, Suite 310, Edina, Minnesota 55439 USA. Copyright ©2010 by Abdo Consulting Group, Inc. International copyrights reserved in all countries. No part of this book may be reproduced in any form without written permission from the publisher. The Checkerboard Library™ is a trademark and logo of ABDO Publishing Company.

Printed in the United States.

Editor: John Hamilton
Graphic Design: Sue Hamilton
Cover Illustration: Neil Klinepier
Cover Photo: iStock
Interior Photo Credits: Alamy, Albert Beirstadt, AP Images, Boston Bruins, Boston Celtics, Boston Pops Orchestra, Boston Red Sox, Cecil Stoughton, Comstock, Corbis, Corey Leopold, Getty, Granger Collection, iStock Photo, J.L.G. Ferris, Library of Congress, Massachusetts Secretary of the Commonwealth, Mile High Maps, Mountain High Maps, New England Patriots, One Mile Up, U.S. Air Force, U.S. National Park Service/Adams Natl Historical Park, University of Massachusetts-Lowell/J.Joy, and The White House.
Statistics: State population statistics taken from 2008 U.S. Census Bureau estimates. City and town population statistics taken from July 1, 2007, U.S. Census Bureau estimates. Land and water area statistics taken from 2000 Census, U.S. Census Bureau.

Manufactured with paper containing at least 10% post-consumer waste

Library of Congress Cataloging-in-Publication Data

Smith, Rich, 1954-
  Massachusetts / Rich Smith.
      p. cm. -- (The United States)
  Includes index.
  ISBN 978-1-60453-656-0
  1. Massachusetts--Juvenile literature. I. Title.

F64.3.S64 2009
974.4--dc22
                              2008051701

Table of Contents

The Bay State

Massachusetts is in the New England region of the northeastern United States. Massachusetts is officially called a commonwealth. It is known as the Bay State because it is near Cape Cod Bay, where the earliest settlements and the Massachusetts Bay Company were first located.

Massachusetts was where the Pilgrims landed and celebrated the first Thanksgiving. Massachusetts is also is known as The Cradle of Liberty. It was where the American Revolution against British rule began.

Some of the most famous universities in the country are in Massachusetts. It also is home to some of the country's most important technology companies. Plus, Massachusetts is the state that invented the chocolate chip cookie, the Boston cream pie, and other treats.

A statue of patriot Paul Revere stands near the Old North Church in Boston. The American war against British rule began in Massachusetts.

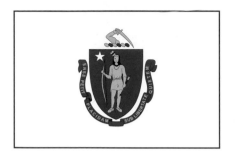

Quick Facts

Name: Massachusetts comes from the name of an Algonquian tribe called the Massachuset.

State Capital: Boston

Date of Statehood: February 6, 1788 (6th state)

Population: 6,497,967 (15th-most populous state)

Area (Total Land and Water): 10,555 square miles (27,337 sq km), 44th-largest state

Largest City: Boston, population 599,351

Nickname: The Bay State

Motto: *Ense petit placidam sub libertate quietem* (By the sword we seek peace, but peace only under liberty)

State Bird: Black-Capped Chickadee

State Flower: Mayflower

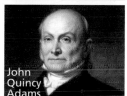

John
Adams

John
Quincy
Adams

John F.
Kennedy

George
H.W.
Bush

State Rock: Roxbury Puddingstone

State Tree: American Elm

State Song: "All Hail to Massachusetts"

Highest Point: Mt. Greylock, 3,491 ft. (1,064 m)

Lowest Point: Atlantic Ocean Shoreline, 0 feet (0 m)

Average July Temperature: 71°F (22°C)

Record High Temperature: 107°F (42°C) at Chester and New Bedford on August 2, 1975

Average January Temperature: 26°F (-3°C)

Record Low Temperature: -35°F (-37°C) at Chester on January 12, 1981

Average Annual Precipitation: 44 inches (112 cm)

Number of U.S. Senators: 2

Number of U.S. Representatives: 10

U.S. Presidents Born in Massachusetts: John Adams, John Quincy Adams, John F. Kennedy, George H.W. Bush

U.S. Postal Service Abbreviation: MA

Geography

Massachusetts is bordered on the north by Vermont and New Hampshire, on the west by New York, on the south by Connecticut and Rhode Island, and on the east by the Atlantic Ocean.

Massachusetts has four geographic regions. First is the Coastal Lowlands in the east. The northern shoreline is rocky. The southern shoreline is sandy, with many salt marshes. Boston Bay, Plymouth Bay, Buzzards Bay, and Cape Cod Bay are the region's four largest coves. Offshore are several pleasant islands in an area called Nantucket Sound. Through the Coastal Lowlands flow the Charles, Mystic, Taunton, and Merrimack Rivers.

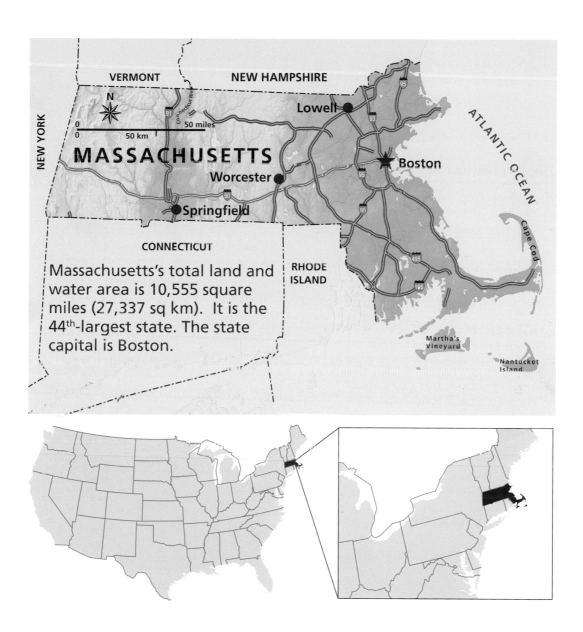

VERMONT   NEW HAMPSHIRE

NEW YORK

N

0   50 miles
0   50 km

Lowell

MASSACHUSETTS

Worcester

Boston

ATLANTIC OCEAN

Springfield

Cape Cod

CONNECTICUT

Massachusetts's total land and water area is 10,555 square miles (27,337 sq km). It is the 44th-largest state. The state capital is Boston.

RHODE ISLAND

Martha's Vineyard

Nantucket Island

The state's second region is the Plateau Region. It begins about 40 miles (64 km) inland from the Atlantic Coast. The highest of its gentle hills is only about 2,000 feet (610 m) above sea level. Found here are many of the state's 1,100 lakes. The Plateau Region extends to the middle of Massachusetts.

Next is the Connecticut River Valley. It has soil that is good for growing crops. The region is famous for its beautiful meadows. They are watered in part by the Connecticut River.

Massachusetts's fourth region is in the far western part of the state. It includes the low-rising Berkshire Hills. Lovers of outdoor beauty come here to see many lakes of clear blue water and wondrous woods.

Fall in the Berkshires.

The Connecticut River cuts across farmland in the Connecticut River Valley. Most of the farms in Massachusetts are found in this region or in the Berkshire Hills Region.

Most farms in Massachusetts are in the Connecticut River Valley and Berkshire Hills Regions. Farms cover about 518,000 acres (209,627 ha). Forests shade about 3.2 million acres (1.3 million ha). Massachusetts has no national forests. But it does have one of the nation's largest systems of state forests, preserves, and parks, on 450,000 acres (182,109 ha) of land.

Climate and Weather

Massachusetts's climate is the continental type. During the winter it is cold. In the summer it is hot and humid.

The waters of the Atlantic Ocean help make the eastern half of the state a little less cold in winter and a little less hot in summer. But both east and west receive about 44 inches (112 cm) of precipitation during the year.

A man fishes in the city streets of Peabody, Massachusetts, after heavy rains flooded the town in May 2006.

Tornados sometimes hit Massachusetts. More common is a dangerous type of storm called a nor'easter. Nor'easters bring fierce winds and heavy rains. They also cause coastal flooding from high tides and big waves. Nor'easters are most common during the winter. One of these was responsible for the Great Blizzard of 1888.

Nor'easters can bring as much as two feet (.6 m) of snow to Massachusetts.

More than 400 people in Massachusetts and neighboring states died because of the storm.

Plants and Animals

Massachusetts has many trees. The most common kinds include oak, pine, birch, and maple. The state also has large numbers of beech, hemlock, and larch trees.

Two kinds of wildflower that seem to bloom everywhere in Massachusetts are the false loosestrife and the Maryland meadow beauty. Aster, goldenrod, lily, and orchid also help make the state's meadows come alive with color.

Loosestrife

The white-tailed deer is one of the state's most familiar animals. Another common animal is the black bear. Also making their home in Massachusetts are the coyote, bobcat, gray fox, skunk, raccoon, porcupine, muskrat, rabbit, beaver, and river otter. Two poisonous snakes native to the state are the timber rattlesnake and the northern copperhead.

A white-tailed deer grazes in a Massachusetts field.

Black Bear

River Otter

Cottontail Rabbit

Wild Turkey

Merlin Falcon

Birds of Massachusetts include the bald eagle, wild turkey, falcon, owl, woodpecker, cardinal, blue jay, sparrow, mockingbird, quail, grouse, ring-necked pheasant, and herring gull. Massachusetts is located along the route that migrating birds travel when they head south for the winter. Among those travelers are the loon and the long-tailed duck.

Lobsters, sea scallops, oysters, shrimp, clams, and mussels are found in large numbers along the coast. The rivers and lakes of Massachusetts contain trout, bass, perch, carp, pickerel, and many other types of fish.

Quahogs (clams), crabs, and conch shells from the waters off the southern coast of Cape Cod.

History

Massachusetts was colonized many thousands of years ago by Native Americans.

In 1602, Bartholomew Gosnold sailed along the Massachusetts coast.

In 1602, English explorer Bartholomew Gosnold sailed along the Massachusetts coast. He named it Cape Cod.

Massachusetts was later visited in 1614 by Captain John Smith, an English adventurer. He named the area New England. Smith wrote a book about his adventures. The book was read by religious people from England who lived in Holland. Smith's book convinced them that they needed to go to the New World as missionaries of the Christian faith. This group was called the Pilgrims.

In September 1620, the Pilgrims set sail aboard a ship named *Mayflower*. They landed at Plymouth Rock in December 1620. During the first winter, nearly half of the group died. But the Pilgrims became friends with Native Americans, who taught them to plant corn. The Pilgrims' first harvest in 1621 was so big that they gave a banquet and invited the Indians as guests. This was one of America's first Thanksgiving Day celebrations.

Ten years later, another group of religious people from England arrived. They were the Puritans. In 1630, they started the Massachusetts Bay Colony and named their little village Boston. Soon, Boston grew to become a major center of trade.

Over the next century, British rulers made life hard for the people of Massachusetts. Laws taking away liberty were one problem. Unfair taxes were another. In 1773, some colonists protested. They boarded three ships and threw valuable English tea into Boston Harbor. This became known as the Boston Tea Party.

Massachusetts colonists, dressed as Native Americans, protested unfair taxes by throwing chests of tea overboard.

Americans' first shots for freedom occurred at the towns of Lexington and Concord.

Great Britain's revenge was to take away more of the colonists' freedoms. But that only made the colonists more angry. In 1775, fighting broke out between colonists and British soldiers at the towns of Lexington and Concord. This was the start of the American Revolutionary War.

The Continental Army won important victories at the Battles of Bunker Hill in 1775, and Dorchester Heights in 1776. The British were pushed out of Massachusetts in 1776.

Many British troops were killed during the Battle of Bunker Hill.

Massachusetts played an important part in creating the government of the United States after the Revolutionary War. In 1788, it became the sixth colony to ratify the United States Constitution and become a state.

By the early 1800s, another revolution came to Massachusetts. This was the Industrial Revolution. Many new factories opened, producing everything from shoes to steam engines.

During the 1840s and 1850s, the United States found itself badly divided. On one side were states that wanted the right to keep slaves. On the other side were states opposed to slavery. It was in Massachusetts that the movement to end slavery began and was strongest.

In the 1860s, the American Civil War finally ended slavery. It was the best of times for Massachusetts. And in the years that followed, the state gave birth to

Wason Manufacturing Company was one of many successful companies in Massachusetts.

many new inventions, discoveries, ideas, and social movements. Today, Massachusetts is celebrated as the home of "Yankee ingenuity."

Did You Know?

- The Pilgrims who landed at Plymouth Rock in 1620 were greeted by a Native American who spoke perfect English. Squanto (also known as Tisquantum) had learned the language 15 years earlier after being taken to England aboard an explorer's ship.

- America's first university is in Massachusetts. It opened in 1636. Today, Harvard University is one of the most famous schools in the country.

- One of the first computers was invented in Massachusetts. It was built by Dr. Vannevar Bush and others in the early 1930s at the Massachusetts Institute of Technology. It was very primitive compared to the computers we use today. It did not even have any electronic parts.

- Bicycle and car tires exist thanks to a discovery made in Woburn, Massachusetts. Rubber is normally gooey, but Charles Goodyear in 1839 stumbled onto a way to make it hard.

People

Theodor Geisel (1904-1991) is better known as children's-book author Dr. Seuss. He wrote and illustrated *The Cat in the Hat, How the Grinch Stole Christmas, Green Eggs and Ham*, and more than 60 other books. He was born in Springfield, Massachusetts.

Robert Goddard (1882-1945) was a scientist who built and flew the world's first rocket that was powered by liquid fuel in 1926. Space shuttle launches and travel from Earth to other planets would be impossible if not for his work. He was born in Worcester, Massachusetts.

Alexander Graham Bell (1847-1922) was the inventor of the telephone. He was born in Scotland and then lived for a time in Canada. At age 25, he moved to Salem, Massachusetts. He worked first as a teacher of deaf children in Boston. Bell's telephone was presented to the world at his Boston laboratory in 1876.

Eli Whitney (1765-1825) helped bring about America's Industrial Revolution. He did that by inventing a machine called a cotton gin. It removed seeds from picked cotton many times faster than doing the job by hand. This made it possible to make clothing at a lower price. He was born in Westborough, Massachusetts.

Leonard Nimoy (1931-) played Mr. Spock on the original *Star Trek* television series. He went on to become a writer and director, as well as a poet and photographer. Nimoy was born in Boston.

John F. Kennedy (1917-1963) was president of the United States from 1961 until his death in 1963. It was Kennedy's dream that America should be the first to put an astronaut on the moon by the end of the 1960s. Americans walked on the moon for the first time in 1969. Kennedy was born in Brookline, Massachusetts.

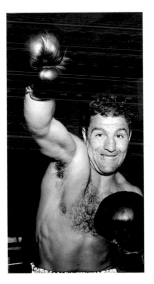

Rocky Marciano (1923-1969) was a champion boxer. He was the only prizefighter to win each and every time he stepped into the ring as a pro. His real name was Rocco Francis Marchegiano. He was born in Brockton, Massachusetts. Marciano was the world champion of boxing from 1952 to 1956.

Cities

Boston is the capital of Massachusetts. It is also the state's largest city. In 2007, Boston had an estimated population of 599,351. Founded in 1630, the city fills up a small peninsula that juts out into Boston Bay. Boston is famous for its schools, colleges, and universities. Boston also is known as a place of scientific research, finance, medicine, and technology.

The second-largest city in Massachusetts is **Worcester.** Its population is approximately 173,966. The city is located in the middle of Massachusetts. Many of the same kinds of businesses and institutions found in Boston are also found in Worcester. Good highways and railroads in and out of the city helped Worcester become a major distribution point for products sold throughout New England.

Union Station in Worcester, Massachusetts. It was originally built in 1911, but fell into disrepair in the 1970s. Cleaned and rebuilt, it reopened in 2000. Today, it is an Amtrak and local bus terminal.

There are many cities across America named **Springfield**. But the one in Massachusetts is the first in the country to have that name. Springfield has an estimated population of 149,938. That makes it Massachusetts's third-largest city. It is located along the Connecticut River in the western half of the state. The game of basketball was invented in Springfield, which is why the city is the home of the Basketball Hall of Fame.

Basketball Hall of Fame.

The first phone numbers in America were those at the homes and businesses of **Lowell,** the fourth-largest city in Massachusetts. In 2007, its population was estimated to be 103,512. Lowell once had more textile mills than anywhere else in the world. Today, it is a center of manufacturing and services.

The city of Lowell in 1850 and today. The city once had more textile mills than anywhere else in the world.

Transportation

Transportation is important to Massachusetts. Cargo ships dock at the state's five major ports. The biggest is the Port of Boston.

The largest airport in Massachusetts is Logan International Airport in Boston. It is used by 26 million travelers each

Logan International Airport is the largest transportation center in New England.

year. Massachusetts has 6 other major airports and about 30 smaller ones for public use.

There are about 35,000 miles (56,327 km) of public roads in Massachusetts. In 2007, the state completed a 3.5 mile (5.6 km) highway tunnel under Boston to ease traffic jams.

Tunnels are nothing new in Boston, home of America's first subway train system. Trains aren't new, either. America's first railroad was built in Massachusetts in 1826. Today, more than 1,200 miles (1,931 km) of tracks crisscross the state.

The Thomas P. O'Neill Jr. Tunnel runs underneath the downtown area of Boston. The tunnel was completed in 2006. It is named after "Tip" O'Neill, Speaker of the House of Representatives for 34 years.

A Red Line Train bringing passengers from Boston towards Cambridge, Massachusetts.

Natural Resources

Cranberries

Massachusetts is the nation's second-largest grower of cranberries. Other crops grown on the state's 7,691 farms include fruits, nuts, and tobacco. Farms also grow corn to feed cows, pigs, and other animals.

From the mines of Massachusetts come crushed stone, construction sand and gravel, and stones cut to specific sizes for the building of homes and offices. Clay, lime, graphite, gypsum, vermiculite, and perlite are other important mineral products from Massachusetts.

Massachusetts does not have enough trees in its forests to make as many wood and paper products as people want. So, extra timber must be cut and brought in from other states.

The most important catches of the Massachusetts commercial fishing industry are lobster, quahogs, and sea scallops.

A shopper finds a live lobster in a Massachusetts market.

Industry

The economy of Massachusetts depends mainly on higher education, biotechnology, finance, health care, financial services, and tourism.

Many of the nation's finest and oldest schools are in Massachusetts. These include Harvard University, Radcliffe College, Massachusetts Institute of Technology, Brandeis University, Tufts University, and Wellesley College.

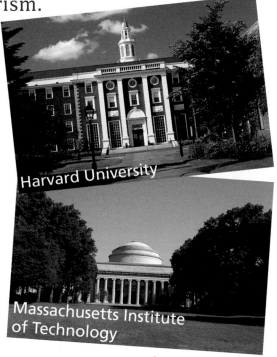

Harvard University

Massachusetts Institute of Technology

Massachusetts is one of the most important biotechnology centers in the world. About 400 biotechnology companies operate in the state. Many of these companies are trying to invent special drugs that someday may save many lives.

Boston's Genzyme Corporation is one of the world's leading biotechnology companies.

At one time in its history, Massachusetts was a mighty manufacturing state. Today, manufacturing is a smaller part of the Massachusetts economy. Things still made in the state include electronic equipment, instruments, industrial machinery, printing and publishing equipment, chemicals, food products, and fabricated metals.

Sports

Some of the best professional sports teams in the world are from Massachusetts. As of 2009, Boston's New England Patriots football team had been Super Bowl champions three times. The Boston Red Sox won Major League Baseball's World Series seven times. The Boston Celtics were National Basketball Association champions 17 times. The Boston Bruins won hockey's Stanley Cup five times.

People in Massachusetts have loved sports for a long time. Basketball was played in America for the first time in Massachusetts in 1891.

Volleyball was an 1895 Massachusetts invention. Started in 1897, the Boston Marathon each year brings at least 20,000 runners to the city for a 26.22-mile (42.2-km) foot race.

Favorite recreational sports in Massachusetts include boating, fishing, hiking, and snow skiing.

The Boston Marathon began in 1897 with 15 runners. Ten of them finished. Today, more than 20,000 runners come from around the world to race. In 2009, the men's winner was Deriba Merga of Ethiopia. The first woman to cross the finish line was Salina Kosgei of Kenya.

Entertainment

The Boston Pops began playing lighter music in 1885. Today, conductor Keith Lockhart leads the orchestra in a cafe-style performance. Listeners sit at tables with refreshments while enjoying the music.

BOSTON POPS

Culture is a very important part of life in Massachusetts. People are especially proud of the Boston Symphony, which is a classical music orchestra. It began playing in 1881. Some players from the Boston Symphony perform lighter music. Their well-known group is called the Boston Pops.

The city of Boston also has opera and ballet companies. Theaters often present plays and musicals that later open on Broadway in New York City.

People who want to look at world-famous paintings go to Boston's Museum of Fine Arts. There are many other types of museums in Massachusetts. Some are about science and history. Others are about industry and sports.

You can come face-to-face with lions, tigers, bears, and elephants at several major zoos in Massachusetts. These include Franklin Park Zoo

An African lion roars at Boston's Franklin Park Zoo.

in Boston and the Forest Park Zoo in Springfield.

Timeline

10,000 BC—Massachusetts is first settled by Native Americans.

1620—Pilgrims land at Plymouth Rock.

1621—The Pilgrims host one of America's first Thanksgiving Day celebrations.

1630—Puritans land at Boston and start the Massachusetts Bay Colony.

1773—The Boston Tea Party.

1775—The battle of Lexington and Concord begins America's fight for independence.

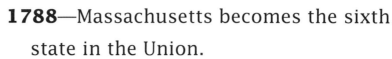

1788—Massachusetts becomes the sixth state in the Union.

1826—The Granite Railway, America's first railroad, is built in Massachusetts.

1876—Massachusetts becomes a technology leader with the invention of the telephone by Alexander Graham Bell.

1926—The Space Age dawns first in Massachusetts with the successful flight of a liquid-fueled rocket.

1961—Massachusetts native John F. Kennedy becomes the youngest man in American history to serve as president.

2004 & 2007—Boston Red Sox win Major League Baseball's World Series.

Glossary

Biotechnology—The use of living organisms to make products, such as hormones or antibiotics.

Civil War—The war fought between America's Northern and Southern states from 1861-1865. The Southern states were for slavery. They wanted to start their own country. Northern states fought against slavery and a division of the country.

Colony—A colony is the establishment of a settlement in a new location. It is often ruled by another country.

Commonwealth—An old word for a government formed to promote the common good of the people. Massachusetts declares itself a commonwealth, but is considered a state by the United States Constitution.

Industrial Revolution—A period of time starting in the late 1700s when machines began taking over many types of work that before had been done by hand.

New England—An area in the northeast United States, consisting of the states of Maine, Vermont, New Hampshire, Massachusetts, Rhode Island, and Connecticut.

Nor'easter—A hurricane-like storm that often strikes the New England states. The name "nor'easter" was given to these storms because they blow into Massachusetts from the direction of the northeast.

Pilgrims—A group of several hundred English men, women, and children who fled their country because the government hated their ideas about religion and worship.

Quahog—A large clam with a hard, round shell found on the Atlantic Coast of North America. It is good to eat and is often used in clam chowder and other foods made with clams.

Revolutionary War—The war fought between the American colonies and Great Britain from 1775-1783. It is also known as the War of Independence or the American Revolution.

Index